SUPER
SURPRISING
TRiViA
ABOUT
NATURAL
DISASTERS

by Mari Bolte

CAPSTONE PRESS
a capstone imprint

Spark is published by Capstone Press, an imprint of Capstone
1710 Roe Crest Drive, North Mankato, Minnesota 56003
capstonepub.com

Library of Congress Cataloging-in-Publication Data is available on the
Library of Congress website.
ISBN: 9781669064824 (hardcover)
ISBN: 9781669071679 (paperback)
ISBN: 9781669064886 (ebook PDF)

Summary: Think you know a lot about natural disasters? Prepare to know
even more about hurricanes, wildfires, earthquakes, and more. You'll be
surprised by how much you'll discover in this totally fascinating book of
natural disaster trivia.

Editorial Credits
Editor: Erika L. Shores; Designer: Heidi Thompson; Media Researcher:
Jo Miller; Production Specialist: Tori Abraham

Image Credits
Alamy: Eddie Gerald, 16; Associated Press, 14; Getty Images: Airphoto
Australia, 7, Boston Globe, 9, filo, 18, GENT SHKULLAKU, 6, gpflman,
17, grandriver, 22, Greg Nature Slade, 23, JOSH EDELSON, 20, OMAR
TORRES, 11, RafalBelzowski, Cover (bottom right), ROBYN BECK, 13, The
Washington Post, 21, Warren Faidley, 5, NASA: JSC, 10; Science Source: Gary
Hincks, 19, USGS, 27; Shutterstock: Adansijav Official, 15 (bottom), ArtMari,
4, Bilanol, 8, David Aughenbaugh, 24, Dieter Kepper, 26, Dmitry Kovalchuk,
25, Eugene R Thieszen, 15 (top), lavizzara, 12, lavizzara, Cover (bottom left),
Marcus Placidus, 29, TDTor, 28, Toa55, Cover (top left), Wichai Prasomsri1,
Cover (top right)

Printed and bound in the USA. 5626

TABLE OF CONTENTS

Words in **bold** are in the glossary.

DID YOU KNO

Natural disasters are severe weather events. They can put people at risk. Floods, hurricanes, tornadoes, and wildfires can be scary. They can cause a lot of damage. What you learn about natural disasters may surprise you!

A hurricane slam: near Miami, Flori

DEEP WATER

Water, water, everywhere—especially during a natural disaster! Around 90 percent of all natural disasters include floods.

Extreme flooding is dangerous. Floodwaters more than 20 feet high can cover houses. It only takes 6 inches of fast-moving water to knock a person over.

Floods cause more death and damage
than tornadoes and lightning.

Not all floods are caused by water. In 1919, 2 million gallons of thick, sticky molasses covered Boston. A storage tank collapsed. The molasses inside made a 50-foot-high wave. It killed 21 people.

IT'S A TWISTER

Tropical cyclones are also called hurricanes or **typhoons**. These giant storms are made up of spinning wind. They twirl at speeds of at least 74 miles per hour.

Hurricane Patricia had wind speeds of 215 miles per hour. It's one of the strongest storms on record.

Soldiers clear trees destroyed by Hurricane Patricia in Mexico in 2015.

Tropical cyclones can be 300 miles wide.
They can drop 2.4 trillion gallons of rain
in a day.

Hurricane Katrina was the most expensive storm ever. It lasted for more than a week in August 2005. It caused $190 billion in damage.

The world's deadliest tropical cyclone happened in 1970. It was called Cyclone Bhola. Between 300,000 and 500,000 people in Bangladesh lost their lives.

Tornadoes are violent twisting columns of air. They stretch from thunderstorms to the ground. About 1,200 tornadoes hit the United States each year.

What city has had the most tornadoes? Oklahoma City, Oklahoma! More than 170 tornadoes have hit the city. It lies in what is known as Tornado Alley.

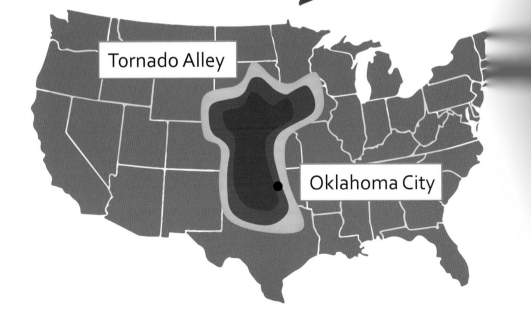

Tornado Alley

Oklahoma City

THE GROUND SHAKES

Earthquakes are all around us. There might be one happening near you right now! Scientists record 500,000 earthquakes every year.

Many earthquakes are tiny. People can't even feel them. But around 100,000 are big enough to be felt. Around 100 of those cause damage.

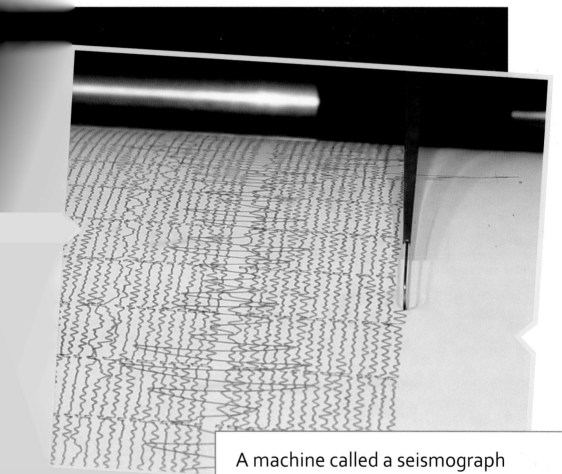

A machine called a seismograph measures movement of the ground.

It is impossible to **predict** an earthquake.

They can happen anywhere at anytime.

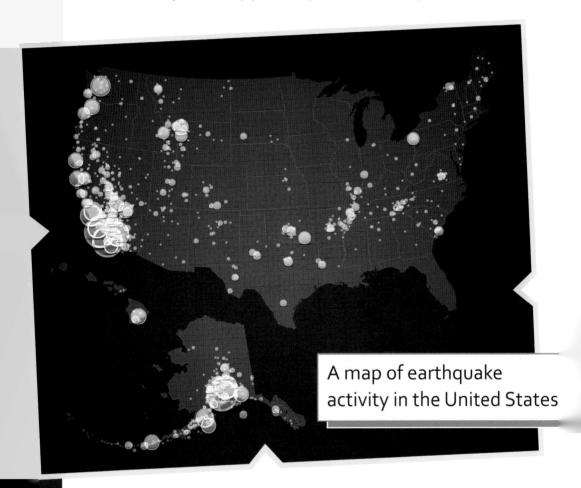

A map of earthquake
activity in the United States

Maybe you should move to Florida
or North Dakota. They have the fewest
earthquakes in the United States.
Alaska and California have the most.

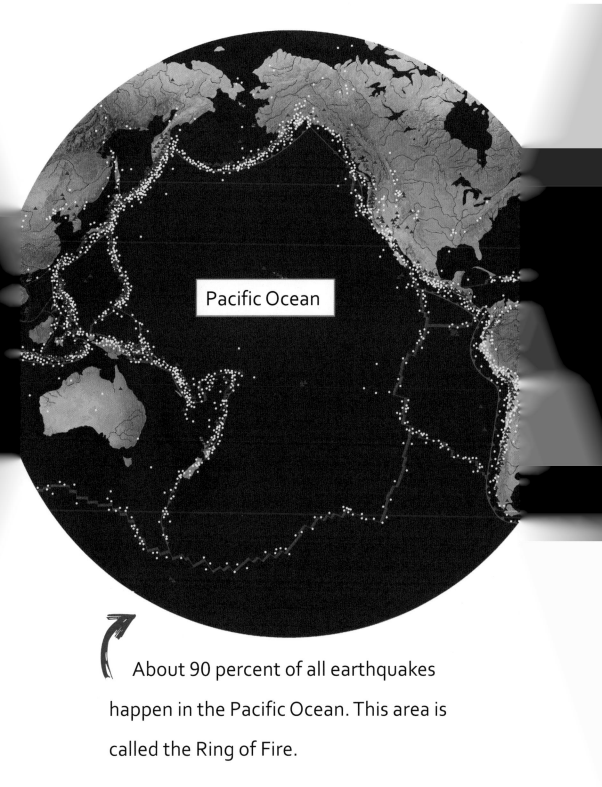

Pacific Ocean

About 90 percent of all earthquakes happen in the Pacific Ocean. This area is called the Ring of Fire.

ON FIRE

Four out of five wildfires are caused by people. Unattended campfires and lit cigarettes are two causes. Some people start them on purpose.

A firefighter during a raging wildfire in California

In 2020, the El Dorado Fire burned in California for 71 days. It was started by a couple who lit a smoke bomb during a party.

Every year there are around
70,000 wildfires in the United States.
They burn 8 million acres of land.

Australian **bushfires** burned in 2019 to 2020. They wiped out more than 46 million acres of land. That's the size of the state of Washington.

Fire trucks aren't the only way to fight fire. Helicopters, **drones**, and robots are also putting out wildfires.

Wildfires are hot. They can reach 2,000 degrees Fahrenheit. That's one-fifth as hot as the sun.

AVALANCHE!

During and right after a snowstorm is the most dangerous time for avalanches. Fresh layers of snow can cause older, built-up layers to break off and slide downhill.

An earthquake triggered the deadliest avalanche. In 1970, two towns in Peru were completely covered by snow. A 1-mile-wide chunk of ice and snow destroyed everything in its path.

It's a **myth** that loud noises cause avalanches. Yell as loud as you want.

Yell, but steer clear! Avalanches can
move at speeds of 80 miles per hour.
That's 10 times faster than a human can run.

Glossary

bushfire (BUSH-fyre)—a fire burning in the Australian wilderness

drone (DROHN)—an unpiloted, remote-controlled aircraft or missile

myth (MITH)—a widely held but false belief or idea

predict (pri-DIKT)—to say what you think will happen in the future

typhoon (tie-FOON)—a hurricane that forms in the western Pacific Ocean

Read More

Bradley, Doug. *20 Things You Didn't Know About Weather*. Buffalo, NY: PowerKids Press, 2023.

Crane, Cody. *All About Hurricanes*. New York: Children's Press, an imprint of Scholastic Inc., 2021.

Murray, Laura K. *The World's Wildest Weather*. North Mankato, MN: Pebble, an imprint of Capstone, 2023.

Internet Sites

Ducksters: Dangerous Weather
ducksters.com/science/dangerous_weather.php

Weather Wiz Kids: Weather Safety
weatherwizkids.com/weather-safety.htm

Index

About the Author

Mari Bolte is an author and editor of children's books on every imaginable subject. She lives in Minnesota, home of some of the most extreme weather in the United States.